GENA McLEAN

FIND YOUR WAY

grow through challenge and change
to live a more meaningful life

Preface 2
Introduction 8
Dedication 14

To find your way...

LIVE AWARE 18

LOOK WITHIN 42

LEAD WITH PURPOSE 66

LET LIFE CHANGE YOU 90

LOVE YOURSELF THROUGH THE PROCESS 114

Conclusion 141
Acknowledgements 142
About the author 145
Seeker & Sage 147
Also by the author 150
Disclaimer 152

PREFACE

I am not a psychologist, counsellor or therapist of any kind.

I do not claim to know the answers but as someone who has lived with debilitating chronic gut pain and difficult-to-diagnose symptoms for more than 30 years, I am very familiar with how challenging life's journey can be.

I have also navigated multiple career moves, small business ventures and interstate relocations, endured unsuccessful pregnancies and a bout of breast cancer and through it all dealt with the crippling self-doubt that comes with the writing territory.

I know uncertainty; I know overwhelm; I know helplessness; and I know them well.

I know what it is to wait, to fall, to lose, to come undone. But I also know what it takes to be patient, to rise, to win and be whole.

But so do you.

My story is your story.

It is the narrative of every human, living or dead.

When we set aside the personal circumstances of every life story, what we're left with is universal — recurring themes of love and loss, joy and disappointment, success and sorrow, triumph and tragedy.

We are each living what American professor of literature and acclaimed author Joseph Campbell coined 'The Hero's Journey'. Every one of us is 'called', every one of us is 'tested' and every one of us has the potential to be 'transformed' by our experiences.

But there is no map — we each have to find our own way.

A diagnosis at age 17 that raised more questions than answers was the catalyst for my Hero's Journey. Little did I know this 'call' to heal the devastating symptoms I was experiencing would be the beginning of a life-long quest that would take me into a deep exploration of the mind-body connection and the human condition.

I have since then devoured thousands of books from the self-help, psychology, spirituality, wellbeing and wisdom literature shelves and undertaken many classes and courses to better understand the relationship between our thoughts, emotions, perceptions and choices and how they influence our wellbeing and our ability to live a meaningful life.

In 2009, the call to write my own self-help work was realised and *Note to Self* was born — a card set and booklet that is still empowering and inspiring people to make authentic choices. But my journey into what it is to be human didn't end there. My health battle escalated activating a bleak period of uncertainty, disbelief and despair that lasted a further 10 years. My career went on hold and I withdrew from my active life, putting all my energy into navigating the crippling symptoms that had no straight answers.

It was then I started writing for a different reason. I needed a safe place to express the intense emotions I was feeling. Every day, I would rant and vent and mourn and plead and pray on paper, acknowledging and releasing whatever I could to try and ease the psychological wounding and profound sense of loss I was experiencing.

Every flare-up and misdiagnosis kindled my desperate yearning to find meaning and understanding from my experience and I would dive even deeper into my pain, writing my way through the ache, the struggle, the suffering until I could find the relief I needed. Insights and revelations would appear on the page, encouraging me to listen, to let go and to trust, transforming this intense time of struggle into one of profound healing and growth.

Every call and test since that first diagnosis has been its own journey: each one an important part of the discovery and healing that is the evolutionary arc of my life, and each an unprecedented voyage with situations and experiences I'd never before encountered. I saw them all as chances to learn — about me, about others, about life, about relationships, about change, about loss, about love — and an invitation to expand my mind and my heart.

My desire to pass on what I learn still burns brightly. In February 2019, I created a coaching business called Seeker & Sage and began sharing the wisdom that had come from my own journey of challenges. I was posting my insights regularly on social media when I noticed a theme emerging. The posts were addressing the struggle we face when we're challenged by change and how we can better manage our approach and response to it. Each was proving to be a timely reminder, not just for me but for my followers too, and I soon realised their timelessness was deserving of a more permanent place to dwell. That's when I decided to create this book.

After all these years of learning from and through life's challenges, I know they have much to teach us. I know first-hand we can emerge from our difficulties not just intact but more open and loving, wiser and kinder, with ourselves and each other, if we see life as a journey and change as an opportunity for growth.

But we only discover the path by walking it, one step at a time, finding our way as we go.

This is everyone's story — the universal underneath the personal; the quest to find the way that best serves our own unique arc of evolution. I can't tell you which way to go or what your way looks like. All I can do is share what has helped me and the countless others I have supported find our way through life's difficulties.

Wherever you are on the journey, it is my hope that this book will prompt insights and bring you the clarity and oomph you need to keep opening, keep changing, keep growing and keep going. May it bring you back to you — the one who knows you better than anyone else; the one with the power to choose and the power to change your experience of life for the better.

INTRODUCTION

We're all travellers on the journey of life. And it's a journey fraught with challenge and change that tests our ability to achieve a happy, meaningful and fulfilling life.

Uncharted territory stirs up confusion and fear. Whether it's voluntarily evoked or comes to us spontaneously, change has the potential to overwhelm us and send us spiralling into self-doubt and apprehension. When we don't know what to do next or which way to turn, a sense of powerlessness can set in, perpetuating more struggle and more suffering.

No wonder we loathe change — it signals a loss of control and raises doubts that we have what it takes to handle the unknown.

But we can't avoid it. Change is a constant in our life — the one thing we can be sure of and the one thing we should expect. Many of us do so, reluctantly and ineffectively, and we suffer for it. Our inability to manage it successfully directly affects our wellbeing — our mental, emotional, physical and spiritual health are all at risk of being depleted and damaged; our self-esteem takes a hit; our relationships deteriorate; our dreams are diminished and the chance to live our most satisfying life disappears.

So how do we navigate the twists and turns of life? How do we handle the bumps, the sharp bends and the dead ends?

To navigate is to find the way, but there isn't one way.

And there is no right way or wrong way — **just your way**.

That's what this book is — a companion to help you find your way.

It encourages a growth mindset — one that is open to change — and the opportunity to journey consciously and compassionately so we can manage change more effectively and love ourselves along the way.

How we view the challenges of life says a lot about how we will cope with them and how successfully we will manage them. While we can't always change the environment or situation we find ourselves in, we can choose our approach and response to it.

We will be tested. We will want to close down when what is needed is to open up and we will turn on ourselves when what we need is to apply patience and care.

This book shows us how we can approach the journey with a willingness to learn from it and grow through it while navigating it consciously and compassionately in our own unique way.

It's a collection of insights, observations and understandings I have taken and made from my own challenges and the many years I have supported clients, students, friends and family with their own difficulties.

What I've noticed over and over is we don't easily embrace change because we doubt our ability to handle it and don't know how to find our way through it. Therefore, changing our relationship with change is vital. And if we want to come through change intact, then changing our relationship with ourselves as we find our way is essential.

Find Your Way is a compilation of reminders distilled from years of journeying with my eyes and heart open — observing, listening, reflecting, learning and letting go. They have helped me overcome confusion, doubt, helplessness and overwhelm, and assisted me to move into acceptance, courage and consciousness while guiding me to face my challenges honestly and with greater compassion.

Five chapters explore what I consider fundamental aspects that help us find our way more consciously and compassionately. They are to: Live aware; Look within; Lead with purpose; Let life change you; and Love yourself through the process.

The entries within each chapter are designed to remind us of what we forget when we're feeling overwhelmed or uncertain. Some will provide a quick prompt while others offer a deeper dive bringing you back to you and to what matters most.

But this is not a book to read — it's a book to use.

Turn to it when you're struggling with change or craving it; if you're feeling lost, overwhelmed, confused, uncertain or afraid; longing for connection with yourself and your life; if you're wanting to find meaning and healing; need to strengthen your self-worth and connect with your inner wisdom; want to meet challenges with awareness so you can navigate them more peacefully, honestly and authentically.

The time you take to explore the contents of this book is up to you. Sometimes you might need a quick reboot; other days you may want to wander the pages until you settle on the message that resonates and then linger there until it soaks in. Just as there is no right way or wrong way to journey, there is also no right or wrong way to use this book. It's a 'companion for the journey', created to travel with you, supporting you as you need it.

Completing many of the entries is an italicised statement starting with the words *May I*. Consider this an invitation to reflect on the personal significance of the message you've just read. It can also be used as an affirmation or intention, opening the door to inner change, inspiring insights or initiating a much-needed mental shift.

As with any book of this nature, there will be times when it is a suitable choice to help you reflect, soothe or readjust. There may also be circumstances where professional help should be sought. In those cases, once the situation has been managed successfully this book may then be drawn from to support the healing process. In any case, trust that you will know how and when to use this book appropriately, but if you have any doubts it is wise to contact a trained professional.

Timing is everything. Insights cannot be forced, healing cannot be rushed and we should not push for resolution. They come in their own time and through various means. It is important to always listen to and honour your own feelings and urgings in relation to your situation and experience.

Remember, there is no right way or wrong way — just your way. And you will find it.

Dear fellow traveller,

The longer I live this journey, the more I realise how important it is for all of us to live it in our own way.

I'm a recovering perfectionist, which means I'm prone to and known for being a bit of a control freak. I have spent the bulk of my life blindly believing there is a right way — the right path — and therefore also a wrong way, to my detriment.

When the goal is perfection there is zero tolerance for mistakes. Striving for 'the right way' for fear of being 'wrong' or judged is no way to navigate life or live it.

My self-esteem has taken a pounding over the years because of this faulty thinking and I have spent many periods of my life feeling discontent, discouraged and disconnected — from myself, from others and from life.

I have let the fear of being 'wrong' rule my choices many times over, which has seen me miss out on countless opportunities for fulfilment and happiness.

But after all the soul-searching I've done, I know ultimately it's about giving ourselves permission to be who we are, where we are, honouring the unique journey we are each on.

It's called self-acceptance. And it's called self-love.

And there isn't one path — no right way or wrong way. We must each find our own way.

So this book is for me as much as it is for you.

May you find your way compassionately and openly, becoming all that you are.

With love,

Gena xo

THERE IS NO RIGHT WAY OR WRONG WAY—
just your way

LIVE
AWARE

Attentive, alert, awake — sensing the inner and outer landscape, making conscious connections, opening up to knowing and understanding more. This is what it means to live aware. This is what we must do if we are to live, really live, every day of our life.

AWARENESS IS YOUR GREATEST ASSET

We cannot live a rich and meaningful life if we are not aware — fully present to what is going on inside and around us.

Nor can we find our way easily if we are wearing blinkers, yet many of us are accustomed to living with this restrictive view. We make choices in the dark, so to speak, trying to find our way without seeing or knowing the whole picture.

Instead, we need to switch on our awareness — remove the blinkers — and see all there is to see so we can find our way consciously, mindfully, deliberately, effectively.

To be aware is to be awake, purposefully looking at and sensing all that is occurring in the inner and outer landscape. Being deliberate with our focus – present and mindful, attentive and observant of what we can and can't see.

Change can be confronting and scary but putting our heads in the sand won't make the change go away.

Without awareness, we can't make authentic choices. We can't even respond, we can only react. And where is the power in that?

Awareness allows us to make conscious choices — authentic choices — that honour our needs and resonate with who we really are and have the potential to be.

Even when we react unconsciously, we can always reflect on our action with awareness and by doing so, learn from it so we can choose differently next time.

Awareness brings choice. It is the doorway to freedom, to change and to you becoming the author of your own life again.

> May I move through this change
> aware of what's going on within
> me and around me.

SHIFT YOUR FOCUS

When we believe we have little or no control over a situation it's natural to feel anxious and impatient or to slip into a pessimistic mindset about what the end result may be.

But how do we want to tolerate the setbacks, the interruptions, the intervals we have no control over?

The answer lies in choosing where to put our attention. Our minds can go down the negative 'what if' path but rather than follow it in the direction of doom, we can redirect our thoughts towards what is positively possible.

We can shift our focus away from the disruption and hold on to the positive possibility that life is for us and the resolution we seek will come at the right time in the right way.

Holding this belief takes us away from unnecessary wariness and worry. We can relax our grip on life and instead work with it.

Everything can be seen as conspiring to aid us in moving through change successfully if we choose to see and believe that life is for us, and keep our focus on what's possible.

Our thoughts have the power to decrease our chance of acceptance, patience and much-needed inner peace. They also have the power to lift us to optimism and hope — to possibility and potential in its highest form.

Where we focus our attention affects the quality of our experience, influencing our mindset, our mood and our ability to handle the difficulties that besiege us.

Fortunately we always get to choose where we place our focus.

> May I keep my attention on what it is I want, rather than dwelling on what I don't want.

ignite your inner seeker

How do you ignite your inner seeker? You start to get curious about who you are and what makes you *you*. You wonder about the world around you and why things are as they are. You start asking questions. And then you trust that the answers will come. But let them come in their own good time. The power is in the asking. Just start asking.

CURIOSITY BREEDS CONSCIOUSNESS

It's natural for us to avoid anything that creates insecurity and uncertainty. Even when change is already upon us, we will do our best to deny it and ignore it. We shut down and act unconscious, hoping we will pass through it relatively unscathed.

But if we are to participate in the unfoldment of our journey we must live aware, and the best way to initiate our awareness is to get curious — to become really interested in what's going on within us and around us.

To be curious is to wonder: to want to know more and to know more deeply.

And curiosity breeds consciousness. We can't help but be drawn closer to what we are curious about.

Curiosity leads to intimacy with the present moment, allowing us to be awake to what's here and what's not — vital information that can help us navigate life with greater awareness and authority.

It invites insights that can enrich and enliven, enabling a more fulfilling experience of life to occur. From that place, solutions may be seen that haven't been seen before. New paths can be revealed, our understanding increases and before we know it, our struggle becomes a time of transformation, all because we are now curious and conscious.

Every experience can be the catalyst for our consciousness to be roused if we let ourselves be curious about what's going on.

We can then find our way, awake and aware, making valuable connections and meaning as we go.

> **May I allow my curiosity to wander and find new insights.**

LISTEN TO LIFE

There's this constant conversation going on between us and the world we inhabit.

Connections, correlations and synchronistic coincidences are unfolding along the way, but do we listen to them?

The people, places, situations, events, changes and challenges in our life are all offering feedback about the choices we're making, the path we're taking, our way of being and the way we're relating, and all can help us find our way.

It's actually a two-way conversation. We supply information through our thoughts and actions and life responds through a multitude of means, giving feedback about all sorts of things — our intention, integrity, direction, effectiveness, priorities. This can help us make more authentic choices aligned with our truth, our purpose and our desires.

Synchronistic and coincidental encounters, where unusual situations and people collide in positive ways, also supply us with information that, if received and interpreted with meaning, can be used to help us navigate.

Evidence is all around us that life is on our side, working for us to support us, guide us, encourage us, inspire us, love us.

But we must look for the signs and be receptive — activate our awareness and be open to their underlying message and the insights they offer, contemplating what they may mean for us personally and our present situation.

To listen to life and pay attention to its feedback is to navigate choice and change consciously.

Start tuning in. There is much wisdom to be gained.

**May I be open to receiving
life's messages.**

be the student

Life has much to teach us. Every situation, experience and event contains the possibility and potential for growth. Just start by being willing to see what needs to be seen, and to know what needs to be known.

THINK WIDER, DEEPER, HIGHER

Sometimes we find ourselves in situations that are baffling to us — we can't see a way out or through and wonder how we got there in the first place. Our thinking can go round and round in circles, leaving us feeling overwhelmed and stuck.

When this happens we need to shift from a narrow field of vision to a more open view — look and think wider, deeper and higher than we have been.

When we open ourselves up to a bigger picture, a broader view, and pursue a deeper contemplation of what we are experiencing, we cannot help but be moved into a more expansive mindset that allows for optimal solutions and meaning to arise.

Rather than pushing for mediocre answers, we mentally give the situation space and distance by asking questions that invite a wider perspective and probe for a higher purpose and a deeper meaning.

Asking questions like, *what is this really about?* and *what is this situation asking of me?* help us think more laterally and creatively. We then have the opportunity to understand in ways that are beyond the logical mind, inviting transformational answers and optimal solutions.

And then, patiently, we wait and watch for the insights to arrive.

The perspective we gain from opening and widening our vision allows us to see and know more and from that place we are well positioned for the next best step to be revealed or for the best healing outcome to be presented — wisdom that our mind couldn't grasp with its limited view.

> May I look for and open to seeing
> and knowing a bigger picture.

STEP IN TIME

Life has its own rhythm and hum — its own cycles and seasons and patterns that fit effortlessly, harmoniously, perfectly, with one another. The trick is to align ourselves with the natural pace of life — to neither defy nor deny any given season or state if we are to live balanced, productive, prosperous lives.

But we don't always walk to the beat of life.

Our ego, thinking it knows best, will initiate a change even if all the apparent signs and circumstances point to keeping the status quo. It will also resist nature's call to change, doing all it can to fight it.

The discord we bring about by refuting life and its mysterious yet perfect timing is detrimental to our wellbeing and our ability to flourish. Unnecessary chaos, confusion and loss are the price we pay when we dispute the natural tempo of life.

Movement requires change. Growth insists on change.

But built in to the cycles of nature are periods of hibernation and inaction, equally balanced and timed with activity and action. The moon will wax and then wane. Birth is followed by death. The tide will ebb and flow.

Trust in the timing that life presents. Honour the metaphorical red and green lights that appear in nature and in relation to others. Respect the timing of unforeseen circumstances and setbacks and use them to help you step in time with life.

> May I be aware of the cycles within and around me so I can flow harmoniously with them.

become aware

When we become aware of our actions and reactions, our choices and their outcomes, our feelings and thoughts and the impact they have on our days and our life, we give ourselves the chance to choose differently and to choose again.

SEE WITH COMPASSION

Awareness is not a harsh light we shine on who we've been or the choices we've made.

The point is not to observe and reflect so that we can judge and blame. The point is to discover and then to see, consciously and clearly, so we can expand our view and make more authentic and supportive choices.

To do this, we must bring compassion to our awareness — not just see what there is to see, but see with the desire to ease any suffering that arises, because the discoveries we make about ourselves and our choices aren't always going to be rosy.

The negative thoughts and harmful self-talk, the destructive actions and inactions, those unhealthy patterns and habits that are running on repeat, will undoubtedly bring up feelings of guilt and shame.

But mindfully and openly, we can carefully unpack and process our experiences without looking to blame ourselves or others.

We find our way through life with our eyes open and our hearts soft — awake to all that is going on inside us and around us while keeping a loving, gentle acceptance for all that arises, as it arises.

> **May I see my situation and choices with compassion and care.**

CLARITY COMES

Uncertainty can send even the most level-headed among us into confusion.

When our direction is disrupted and our best-made plans are thrown into disarray, we can feel bewildered, disorientated and at an absolute loss as to where to go or what to do next.

Clarity is what we want and we'll do anything to get it. But it can't be forced.

Putting pressure on ourselves and our circumstances to become clear will not bring us the clarity we so desperately want and need. Making decisions out of fear has never been fruitful or brought the relief and sense of peace we are hoping for.

We must realise that clarity comes when we are receptive to receiving.

It will not come through will or might, influential ability or perceived degree of control. Even the intensity of the pain it is inducing or the time-sensitivity of the situation will not increase our chances of getting clear.

We can't think our way there, either.

Clarity is not necessarily rational or logical in its timing or means of arrival.

It will only come when we stop the problem-solving merry-go-round and let go of sorting our way toward the solutions we seek.

When we shift from thinking to receiving mode, we provide an opportunity for answers to drop in, resolutions to appear and possibilities to be exposed.

Recognising the confusion we're experiencing as a sign to consciously release the issue and all the mental anguish that goes with it will clear the way and make vital space for clarity to come.

May I clear the way for clarity to come.

LOOK
WITHIN

You know what you need and
you know who you are. Open up
to the wisdom and truth within you
and trust what you feel, hear,
sense and see.

YOUR INNER SAGE KNOWS

Life is not always easy to navigate, especially when we're caught in a storm of psychological distress and upheaval. Even when we want to instigate change, we don't always know how or where to begin.

Fortunately, we are all equipped with a navigation system that will help us get back on track or guide us to a new path. But we must look within to find it.

There is a part of us that is wise beyond our years, a part that knows what we need, who we are, and what to do next, but the logical mind doesn't rate it. It prefers to make decisions based on hard evidence and facts, favouring reason and rationality over instinct and intuition. It's far more comfortable drawing on intel derived from research and proven findings.

But the wisdom within — our inner sage — knows.

Connecting with and listening to our inner guidance system is a powerful and authentic way to live.

By tuning in to all of the senses, we discover vital information about what we need and want, who we are, what we're feeling and which direction to travel.

It's natural and valuable to turn to others for help, but to totally rely on them for knowledge and solutions is to deny our own empowerment, understanding and growth.

Listen to your heart and your gut. Pay attention to what you are feeling and sensing — intuitively, emotionally, physically and spiritually — then use this information to guide you as you find your way.

To connect within and search inside yourself for answers is to honour and love yourself during whatever transition you're going through.

May I go within for the answers I seek.

BACK YOURSELF

So many of us can easily step into the supporter role, championing others when they are struggling, but we often desert ourselves in our own time of need.

We doubt our abilities, so much so that we can turn against ourselves, lashing out with harsh self-talk and unconscious reactions that reject our needs and damage our already fragile sense of self. Instead of supporting who we are, where we're at and what we're trying to achieve, we end up devaluing, undermining and eroding our self-esteem and our efforts.

When we're facing a challenge, we need to reinforce our allegiance to ourselves — be loyal and devoted to our wellbeing, our path and our plight. But we frequently fall victim to our fears.

If we are going to navigate change successfully, coming through it not just intact but richer for the experience, we need to believe in and back ourselves.

You need to know that no matter how high the mountain or slippery the slope, you're with you, and for you, supporting yourself all the way. You need to be the champion for your own cause, believing in your ability to make it through.

You need to tell yourself you will find a way no matter how discouraging the odds are because your voice, thoughts, feelings and beliefs about you will make all the difference to how you make it through this transition.

There is no one who needs your belief and backing more than you.

> **May I believe in myself and be loyal to my cause and my efforts.**

gather wisdom

Don't you just love those aha moments when you get a sudden insight or revelation — a recognition, a burst of clarity, a download, that much-needed discovery leading to understanding, acceptance and oftentimes the next right action.

Treasure them. They are a gift from your intuition.

Use them. They can propel you forward and help you find your way.

CALL ON COURAGE

Fear is a natural response to change, but it's how we view it and what we do with it that matters the most.

When fear arises it can trigger more fear, creating a vicious cycle. The result: a disempowering paralysis affecting our ability to think clearly and take the next appropriate action.

Combatting and controlling fear is not necessarily the answer, but changing our relationship with it is.

We don't want to be afraid of fear — we want to see it as a sign to activate courage, which is the antidote to fear.

The key is to think and act with strength and determination and to persevere despite the fear, the pain, the difficulty we're facing. It is to dig deep and find within us what is needed to bravely move forward.

This doesn't mean we must first find the courage so we can then act. Courage will come from and through the action we take.

We're all going to feel fear as we journey through life, about all sorts of things — we're human! But if we recognise it as a prompt to enact the courage we need to move through our challenges, then we are well on our way to working through change effectively.

Beyond the fear is the outcome, the desire, the goal you are wanting.

Call on courage to help you get there.

> May I call on courage when I feel fear and use it to help me move through change.

DIG DEEP

The journey can be demanding, asking more of us than we've ever given before.

And when it does, our first reaction is often one of doubt. We think we don't have what it takes to make it through.

We question ourselves and retreat under the weight of the unknown. We let our past experiences dictate what we can and can't handle now, all the while sensing that the known, our comfort zone, is no match for the change we are facing.

But buried beneath our habitual responses and behaviours is a reservoir of potential — a wellspring just waiting to be realised. And because we're creatures of habit and like to cling to comfort, this untapped resource remains dormant until change comes along.

The thing is, we don't really know what we're capable of until we're pushed and stretched — until differing circumstances force us to dig even deeper.

Qualities we already revere are enhanced under the pressure and previously unknown positive attributes can be revealed and drawn forth.

But we must dig deep to discover them.

We must let life have its way with us, yielding to its demand on our evolution to become more fully who we came here to be.

There is much value to come through and from change.

We may not be aware of what is needed yet, or what we're being asked, but we will find it if we dig for it, and dig deep.

May I dig deep drawing on the strength and wisdom that dwells within.

WITHIN EVERY STRUGGLE IS A *strength* WE DIDN'T KNOW WE HAD

TRUTH BE TOLD

Change is definitely a disruptor, bringing chaos great and small to our outer circumstances and our inner world. Truths we didn't know existed can surface, shocking us with their aptness and clarity, some delivering great relief and comfort while others will send us into fear and hiding.

But we cannot navigate life successfully if we don't tell ourselves the truth about what we want, how we feel, who we are, where we're at and what needs to change.

Besides, how will we ever live our happiest and most meaningful life if we continue to deceive ourselves?

With an intention of compassion and our complete awareness, we must admit to ourselves honestly and sincerely what it is we are seeing.

We speak the truth about our feelings and about what's going on for us. No holding back.

Whatever comes up — insights into old wounds, heartfelt longings, our deepest fears — we tell the truth about.

Lasting, fulfilling change can only happen when we are honest with ourselves.

If we are to live authentically and with integrity we must tell ourselves the truth and live by it. And if we want strong relationships based on trust with people we can be honest and intimate with, then we must first and foremost be honest with ourselves.

Expressing our truth may upset the applecart, but if we don't, we rob ourselves of the life we came here to live.

Whatever truth you have discovered is worthy of your validation. Honour yourself by making room for it.

May I be honest with myself and tell the truth about what I'm experiencing.

HOLD ON TO HOPE

Complications and chaos have the capacity to fray our nerves, inspire despair and leave us wondering if there is a way forward, out or through. Thoughts of anguish overwhelm our ability to patiently hold on — we lose heart and we lose hope.

When this lasts for days, weeks or months we can lose sight of any sign of light. The tunnel has no end and our hope is lost.

During tough times it's common to hold on to the pain, the trauma, the terror and let go of the very thing that will buoy us: hope.

Hope is like a lantern in a long, dark night. Resolutely, humbly, it rouses optimism and faith, encouraging us to keep our sights set on the best possible outcome.

It encourages us to stay focused on what we want, rather than what we don't want, reinstating the belief and expectation that good will come, help will arrive, and healing will happen, no matter how disheartening our present circumstances seem.

With hope we can loosen our grip, let go of the struggle and let our thoughts and spirits be revived with positivity and possibility.

And it's always available — all we have to do is choose it and hold on to it. Our circumstances may remain but with hope we have a better chance of navigating the challenge with the openness and energy we need to see it through.

Whatever challenge you are confronted with, let go of the hurt, the despair, the struggle, but don't let go of hope.

> May I hold on to hope with both hands as I navigate this change.

you are enough

Along the way it's easy to get trapped into thinking and believing that we are not enough: that we are lacking in some quality or skill that renders us insufficient, incomplete, unacceptable and unworthy.

The faulty thinking we buy into tells us we're not smart enough, good enough, lucky enough, clever enough, tall enough, creative enough, talented enough, successful enough. Enough!

You are enough. Exactly as you are, how you are, and who you are.

This doesn't mean we don't continue on our path of evolution — growing, shedding and becoming. That will always be. That is the nature of nature.

It means that at every stage we are enough exactly where we are.

RESET AND RENEW

Feeling stuck, overwhelmed, confused or downhearted may be a sign that old, limiting beliefs are on repeat in your mind, drowning out thoughts of positivity and love, causing you to falter and doubt yourself and your plans.

As feeling and sensing beings, we can easily become overloaded with unhealthy thoughts and emotions.

The truth is, we hold on — to the small hurts as well as the big pains — to our detriment.

Before we know it, there's a toxic cocktail of bitterness, resentment, helplessness, regret, anger, hatred, guilt and shame poisoning our mood, our behaviour, our choices, our relationships and our physical health.

Studies have shown the powerful and positive healing effect acceptance, compassion and forgiveness can have on our stress levels, let alone our capacity to feel more contentment, gratitude and love — for ourselves and others.

Wherever you are on the path, your mind and heart need the chance to release and reset.

Let go of whatever is holding you back from living, being and achieving all that you desire. Clear the beliefs that don't serve you anymore. Bin the thoughts that trash your confidence and your courage and keep only what will lift you, inspire you, encourage you and empower you.

> May I tend to my inner world so I can reset and renew my heart and mind.

FIND FAITH

The journey can be rough, knocking us around with its unexpected obstacles and turbulent terrain. Uncertainty creeps in, destabilising us emotionally, psychologically and spiritually, causing us to lose faith — in ourselves, in a brighter future, even in life itself.

We've all faced testing times when a drastic change in circumstance is desired and thankfully, delivered. We kept the faith and it paid off.

But what about the times when we cannot alter the terrain because the change that has swept through is irreversible, done, final? What then?

These are the times we must develop an unwavering faith. We must become steadfast and relentless, not on a particular outcome, but on trusting we will get through and we will be helped to get there.

We must believe goodness will emerge despite the devastation and that we will find a new way to live and be.

It can seem like an impossible leap to make, but it is during these very tough times when our rational mind can't fathom a way forward that we must summon and commit to faith and rely on it to help us find our way.

> May I journey with faith, trusting that life will support me as I find my way.

LEAD WITH PURPOSE

Purpose is not just about the big picture or the meaningful goal. Every day we have the opportunity to live and lead with purpose.

LIVE WITH PURPOSE

When we're going through a transition we naturally want to focus on the end result, but this can inadvertently make the days between here and there feel meaningless and insignificant.

Purpose is not just about the big picture, the meaningful goal or desired outcome we are working towards.

Every day we have the opportunity to live with purpose.

Every task, every job, every encounter can be met and executed intentionally and purposefully.

To live with purpose is to consciously engage with every experience, each moment, as though it really matters. Because it does! It's the only moment we can live — the only moment we have.

Why not make it matter by giving it the attention and importance it deserves — you deserve! This life is yours, and what you bring to each and every one of your experiences has the capacity to turn a time of worry and waiting into one of wonder, meaning and connection.

When we approach everything we do as important and everyone we connect with as valuable, our days are suddenly, miraculously transformed. The mundane becomes meaningful and we begin to experience a richness and depth in our life we thought could only come from attaining our big-picture purpose.

Bring your being to your doing and live each moment with intention. Be deliberate daily, no matter what the task, and your life will again be purposeful.

> May I live with purpose, approaching every situation with the importance it deserves.

JUST DO TODAY

The journey can be overwhelming, especially when it's rife with turbulence and disorder. Our minds race ahead trying to grasp what our future will look like and how we might navigate each day to get there.

Even when we have embarked on change willingly, it's easy for us to get carried away and already be working on what needs to happen tomorrow, and next week, and next month — even next year!

We must plan, yes, and have goals, but we must also live one day at a time.

Unfortunately, many of us have become proficient at living tomorrow and the next day and the next week in our minds today, and then wonder why we feel so tired, overwhelmed and disheartened.

To journey successfully, with our wellbeing intact, we must adjust our focus accordingly. Take one day at a time, one step at a time, even one moment at a time — whatever we need to break the journey down into mentally manageable chunks. We can't do any more than that anyway. In fact, we can't do any more than this moment, this breath, right now.

This journey is not about ticking actions off a to-do list. It's to be lived daily.

And if we are to be our most potent, conscious and capable selves, we must focus our attention on the now, and do what's right in front of us. Take the very next breath and the very next step and just do today.

> May I bring myself back to this day, this moment, and live it as fully as I can.

bring your presence to the present

We're all running a metaphorical marathon but the only way to make it to the finish line is to focus on the present moment.

ACCEPT WHAT IS

None of us like dealing with disruption or disaster.

Our most human response is to slip into denial about unwanted situations. We'd rather not go there so we do our best to reject or repress what is, which only leads to more difficulty, more frustration and more suffering.

The antidote is acceptance but none of us want to do that either. Saying 'yes' to something painful seems counterintuitive and fundamentally wrong, but we must learn to if we are to move through our experiences consciously and compassionately.

The thing is, acceptance is never a judgment. It's not a like or a dislike. It's a neutral acknowledgment that what is, is. It is an unbiased seeing that does not condone nor overlook; a recognition that what is happening is happening.

Miraculously, once we're at that place we find a calm we didn't think possible.

The inner chaos subsides and choices become available that we didn't have access to before. We are again standing in our power, responding to life with all the self-authority we have at our disposal.

Acceptance is not backing down, nor is it saying we have to put up with what we are experiencing. Rather, it puts an end to the resistance and denial that keeps us stuck and in fear. It is the doorway to possibility and the pathway forward.

Acceptance is not always easy but it is necessary if we are to transform our suffering and live a more empowered life.

> May I be willing to accept *what is* so that I can open myself to the path ahead.

MEANING MATTERS

Shocks and challenges along the way can cause us to question why. Why me, why us, why this, why now? While these questions are natural — we all want answers as to the origins of our pain — they are not necessarily helpful in determining the meaning behind our situation.

Instead, we're better off looking for and assigning our own meaning that honours our involvement and brings understanding to our minds and healing to our hearts.

Because the meaning we give to our experiences will decide whether we are an unconscious victim who is powerless to effect any change, or whether we are a conscious responder who is actively participating in creating their most healthful and fulfilling life.

This choice is always ours.

With a mindset that is open to the growth and healing within change, we can make our own meanings out of our difficulties and integrate them into our life's story, bringing the peace and healing we need to move forward.

When change makes no sense and we cannot grasp it, we must get involved with the struggle and make it mean something valid, constructive, purposeful, if we are to stop the spiral into blame and hopelessness and find a place for our minds and hearts to rest.

It's the meaning we give to our experiences that makes all the difference.

Change has much to teach us. We can't always alter the outcome, but we get to decide what it ultimately means.

> **May I assign my own meaning and value to this change.**

your life needs you

If we want to live a rich and happy life, we must show up for ourselves. We must dare to be brave and vulnerable, conscious and committed — connected to ourselves, to our path and to life. Our fulfilment depends on it.

When we fall into the trap of living for others, we inadvertently put ourselves last. Our needs and dreams go unattended and we wonder where the longing and emptiness comes from. Resentment builds from the self-neglect and before we know it, we are miles away from the happiness we crave.

This is why your life needs you — not just to care about it, but to participate in it wholeheartedly.

You can't live a fulfilling life without *you*.

STRENGTHEN YOUR WHY

Obstacles will appear whether we go in search of change or are subjected to it. And when they are intense and overwhelming, we can wonder *how* we are ever going to find our way and make it through.

Questions that start with *how* rarely bring us the answers we so desperately want when we are navigating change. Even when we think we have figured out a way, unforseen difficulties can cause delays that threaten our ability to hang in there and keep the faith.

Fortunately there is a remedy to potential hopelessness and poor resilience — it is to remember and strengthen your *why*.

Your *why* is your purpose for undertaking change in the first place, or your reason and determination for surviving it. It is what caused you to action change or the resolution you must reach if change was thrust upon you.

It's your original intention; your rationale and motivation; your aim and the persistence required that will, if recalled and reinforced, give you the energy you need to keep going despite the setbacks and the journey still to take.

When you start to wonder *when is this transition ever going to end*, just remember your why. Clarify and solidify your reason, your purpose, your goal, and you will find a way to live and grow through any difficult *how*.

Rarely is the journey a sprint. When we've already come quite a distance, we can run out of puff and perseverance, doubting *how* we will continue.

But we don't have to know *how* — we just have to remember *why*.

> **May I reinstate my why as I move through this challenge.**

MAKE NO MISTAKE

Journeys are littered with trials and tribulations. We will be tested and we won't always make our way through without a misstep or a mistake.

We are human — we are not infallible. But how we view our errors and our slip-ups makes all the difference to our sense of self-esteem and to whether we will keep moving forward.

So many of us are guilty of blaming and shaming ourselves when we make a mistake.

We aim for a version of situational perfection and when our actions fall short, producing a less-than-desired outcome, we go to war, berating ourselves for our inadequacies and our poor choices.

But if everything can be learnt from, then there's no such thing as a mistake.

Our 'mistakes' are then viewed as valuable sources of important information — useful aids in helping us find our way more effectively.

Every choice produces an outcome that will either take us closer to or further from what we want.

When seen this way, a mistake is a way for us to become clearer about our wants and needs and the resolution we are seeking. We can then stop judging ourselves as good or bad, right or wrong, and instead weigh up the result as effective or ineffective, working or not working.

If we are to continue on the path with our self-worth intact, we must keep ourselves out of the firing line. No more self-criticism or personal shaming when we make a mistake, just an honest review of its effectiveness and the freedom to choose again.

> **May I see my mistakes as separate from me and use them to learn from.**

THE GIFT MAY
BE HIDDEN, BUT
IT'S THERE—
keep digging

LOOK FOR THE GOOD

This is not about being grateful, although it will lead you to that state. Nor is it about putting a positive spin on and thereby minimising what you are going through.

It's a gentle wake-up call reminding you that some days, some times, despite the turmoil you're experiencing, it helps to actively look for the good that is innately present in every situation.

Life continues to show us that no matter how difficult, troubling or traumatic things can be, there is always something to be gained from the experience.

You may not see it straight away — it can take time for the dust to settle — but the moment you start looking for it, or even entertaining the thought that something 'good' could come from something so 'bad', you are on the road to healing.

Some circumstances are catastrophic making it hard to see how any good could come from such an event.

Even change that is welcomed can contain its own dark periods. But keep looking.

The good may be disguised or so deeply buried amid the difficulty that you think it doesn't exist. But it's inherent in everything and all it takes is your willingness to see it.

Finding the good won't replace the loss you've suffered but it will refresh your spirit, give you hope and help you keep going.

> **May I look for and find the good inherent in this situation.**

YOU ARE THE SOLUTION

It's a fundamental truth we so easily forget, especially when we're feeling disillusioned: that no matter where we're at or what we're facing, we're always part of the solution because we always get to choose our response.

What we think, how we act, what we focus on, who and what we forgive, what we do next – it all comes down to choice and the choices are always ours.

The fact is, we each have the power and ability to choose how we respond to what is unfolding. Even when we react unfavourably, we are still capable of reflecting and making a different choice that will take us closer to what we want.

This is the birth of empowerment: we are delivered from victimhood and helplessness when we remember we are the authority in our life.

Our mindset, our perception, our view, our interpretation are all changeable and choosable, and they directly affect what an experience will mean to us, how we talk to ourselves about it and how we navigate our way through it.

The journey is made up of a series of changes and the choices we make in response to those changes. Even though we can't always control the changes that occur, we can face each choice as it arises, consciously and honestly, honouring our own unique process, participating as best we know how.

The quality of our life is a direct reflection of our daily choices. We can change our life and who we become, one choice at a time.

> May I remember that I always have the power to choose and the power to change.

LET LIFE CHANGE YOU

If we let it, life will show us what
we're really made of. It will help
us become more of who we really are.
We're meant to change.
We're meant to grow. We're meant
to live the fullest life possible and
we can — if we let life change us.

CHANGE IS AN OPENING

Life is always changing but we don't necessarily want to change with it. We fear what it may bring or do to us and the uncertainty cripples our ability to work with it. We'd rather cling to what we know — to what feels safe and familiar — even if it makes us feel unhappy and unfulfilled.

When we do this, we resist the inherent growth that is available through every obstacle and so-called issue.

We forget it's natural to change — that life is change and we're meant to change with it.

Opportunities to change often come disguised as illnesses and accidents, job dissatisfaction, relationship breakdowns, housing issues, financial crises, family upheavals, significant birthdays, the death of loved ones, environmental disasters and spiritual longings.

These journeys within the journey can leave us reeling and grasping for answers. But no matter how big or small the change, it is our relationship with it that matters the most.

The meaning we assign to it and what we tell ourselves about it has the power to send us into further fear, anxiety and panic, or into a mindset that is open and accepting of what is a much bigger picture.

We are all at risk of suffering from change but when we see it as an opening for valuable learning and transformational healing to take place, then we are not just surviving life, we are thriving.

This is true change. This is the change the world needs each of us to make.

> **May I be open to this change
> and what it's asking of me.**

LET YOURSELF GROW

Some changes can be seen as annoying disruptions to be endured then put behind us. Gritting our teeth, we go through the motions and do what needs to be done, while wishing whatever we are going through would be sorted so we can get on with life.

It's a coping mechanism we've all employed in challenging times and a natural response to change, but when we do this we disfavour ourselves, closing off from the growth and healing to be had through any situation, big or small.

We don't need to know how we'll be transformed or what will come from tough times, but if we can entertain the notion that every so-called problem, difficulty, setback and disruption contains the opportunity for a greater version of ourselves to be revealed, then we can let ourselves grow through what we're experiencing.

To decide and declare the change we are experiencing is happening for us rather than to us is how to develop a growth mindset.

It opens us up to the possibilities and benefits that change offers, and then with awareness, we can move through change attuned to the opportunities for personal evolvement and healing.

Growth may masquerade as difficulty and disaster, but we don't just have to go through them — we can grow through them.

Let go of fixed ideas about your identity and allow yourself to be moved, moulded, pruned and expanded. Let yourself grow and become more of the person you came here to be.

> May I grow through this change becoming more of who I truly am.

EVERY CHALLENGE
BRINGS WITH IT
THE OPPORTUNITY
TO GROW MORE
FULLY INTO OUR
best self

LEARN YOUR WAY

The journey, with all of its changes and challenges, is actually an unprecedented voyage for every one of us.

No matter how many years we've been at it there will be terrain — situations and circumstances — we've never found ourselves in before. And because we're all unique in our biology and our biography, we will navigate in our own way.

Others can model and demonstrate, instruct and guide, but ultimately it is up to us to find our way, our way, learning what works and what doesn't as we go.

Learning implies movement and growth, reminding us that we are all a work in process. We need to be compassionate with ourselves and hold back from judging our choices as right or wrong, good or bad, positive or negative — because it's all learning and it's all progress.

Not only are we learning as we go, we are unlearning. Unhealthy and outdated patterns, beliefs, goals and ways of being are made clear when we walk through life with the awareness and intention to learn as we go.

We're all on a journey, learning to live, learning to let go, learning to love — ourselves and each other. All at our own pace and in our own unique way.

> **May I be willing to let go as well as learn my way.**

RELEASE AND RECEIVE

We can't always control where the journey will lead us, or the length of time it takes to reach our anticipated destination.

We will have a plan of how we want things to go, but under the strain of the unknown we can unconsciously tighten our grip, turning our preferred outcome into a command that unintentionally restricts our prospects for the best possible and speediest resolution.

With pressure mounting we refuse, deny, defend, demand — anything to get our way and put an end to the uncertainty. We fight back, stand firm, persist, resist — anything but loosen our grip, let go and surrender.

It's natural to resist change, but this creates an unwelcome barrier, closing us off from the space needed for solutions to arrive. We become so intent on ending the struggle that we narrow our mind and its view, which leads to more worry and unnecessary suffering.

The sooner we realise our holding on is hindering our progress, the quicker we can let go and allow for the way to unfold.

Surrendering is not about giving in, succumbing to failure or admitting defeat. Nor is it a sign of weakness. It is about having the strength to give up any resistance to what is, so we can release our expectations and receive what will be the best way forward and through.

Space is made for solutions to enter. Clarity has the chance to come. Inner peace becomes possible. And our inner sage can again be heard.

When we release the struggle and loosen our grip, we let the receiving begin.

> **May I release any resistance so I can receive whatever it is I need.**

begin again

The journey asks that we commit. It requires perseverance to see it through, but in order for us to make it to our destination we must begin — again and again and again.

BREAK THROUGH

Breakdown mode. It's that place where nothing looks the same and everything feels different, strange and difficult — when life as we have known it is no more.

We don't like it. In fact we fear it immensely, but if we can see that a breakdown is actually a breakthrough we can change our relationship with it and ourselves as we find our way through it.

Breakdown mode will always clear away what's no longer needed and reveal what is. Whether it stems from an internal struggle with our present circumstances or is triggered by an external event, it is an invitation to let go, heal and change the way we do life.

In order to break through, we must first be shown what needs to be broken down.

With compassionate awareness we can see what outdated patterns, beliefs and behaviours need to be transformed so we can live in more healthy, authentic and fulfilling ways.

It's an opportunity to tend old wounds, healing and clearing the way for a new direction, or clarifying and strengthening us as we tackle the next leg of the path we're already on.

Whatever the situation, breaking down is always a journey of wholeness.

It's not easy to accept, but if we can see it as a valuable process that dismantles our old ways of being and doing so we can break through to the new, then we can go gently with ourselves and allow space for the goings to go and the comings to come.

> May I see this breaking down as
> a transforming break through.

MAKE PEACE WITH THE PROCESS

This life is a process, but it's not linear or one-directional.

It's an ever-changing collaboration and integration of actions that have us opening and closing, expanding and contracting, awakening and falling back to sleep.

Something triggers us. Some tragedy, an illness, an accident, a death prods us to wake up – to the truth, to ourselves, to life. And when we do, we expand our awareness and grow in consciousness. We become more open and accepting. We see things differently and we are changed, for the better, for a time.

We then travel along with this new aperture of awareness until the next trigger and then the process begins again.

Or we close down, slowly losing consciousness until bam! Another initiation propels us to open and grow again.

Expansion and contraction. Opening and closing. Waking and sleeping. It's the nature of the journey.

Knowing this, we can stop criticising ourselves for our so-called mistakes and unconscious reactions. We make peace with the process, trusting and accepting the journey as it is.

There will be times when we yield great evolutionary gains, making the most of the opportunities for growth when they arise. There will also be times when we navigate with our eyes closed, resisting the call to wake up. But that doesn't mean we're doomed and stuck, it just means we're human.

It's all part of the process of change and growth — of learning and unlearning as we expand and become more conscious. And we're all doing it at our own pace, in our own way.

> **May I make peace with the process and my progress.**

THIS JOURNEY
IS ONE OF
evolution.
IT'S NOT ABOUT
ARRIVING—
IT'S ABOUT WHO
YOU BECOME
ALONG THE WAY.

Sometimes change is sparked by adversity. Other times, the familiar frustrates us and we realise it's time to find a new groove.

Regardless of its origin, we can't ignore the call. We must step bravely toward the unknown and embark on the journey of becoming.

But it's not something we can strive for, nor can it be rushed.

It's what happens when we let life change us — let it move us and shift us and shape us into the person we came here to be — one challenge, one choice at a time.

THE PURPOSE IN THE PAIN

The path is littered with problems.

Pain and suffering surface through many portals, devastating us, overwhelming us, pushing us to our human limits, leaving us bewildered as to what and why and how.

These troubling times are a part of life, but they are not without purpose.

Our hardships and struggles are never in vain.

Every time we are faced with loss we are pushed out of our comfort zone. Knowing there is purpose to our pain can help us find the courage to bravely step into that unknown.

Every obstacle, every setback, every difficulty encountered has an essential function. It is an awakener — a gateway to healing and growth, drawing forth that which enables us to live more fully, more deeply, more consciously, more compassionately.

No one can tell us the exact purpose of our pain — it is up to each of us to discover for ourselves.

For some, relationships that have been hurt have the chance to heal. For others, it is about reconnecting with the heart and bringing dreams to life. Some find healing for old wounds and others get the permission they need to make a radical relocation.

Sometimes it is only when we find ourselves in unfamiliar territory, afraid, lost, confused and forced to find new ground that we will unearth the healing we didn't know we needed and make the changes we would otherwise have been too scared to make.

When the familiar and the safe seem to vanish, we have a golden opportunity to discover things about ourselves we didn't know and acquire a deeper appreciation for the life we have been given.

This is how we heal. This is how we evolve.

> **May I find purpose in this pain that will lead to healing and growth.**

WASTE NOTHING

No matter how difficult, troubling or traumatic things can get, there is always something to be learnt from the experience.

Every happening, encounter, circumstance, setback, challenge, heartbreak, achievement — no matter how big or small — can be used to gain ground, moving us closer to what we want and to becoming more of who we truly are.

But some situations are easier to learn from and grow through than others.

Whether the conditions are simple or complex, we must refrain from forcing the wisdom into being.

Change is a process, as is learning and growth. And every change will have its own nature, its own speed, depth and intensity — none of which are ours to manipulate or manoeuvre.

Rather, what will serve our evolution best is to be open, aware and attentive to what emerges through the transition we are navigating.

We adopt a growth mindset, looking out for the learnings inherent in everything and integrating the insights and healing into our way of being when they come.

When we know deep down that the underlying purpose of every experience is for us to evolve psychologically, emotionally and spiritually, we waste nothing. We then live our life fully and with a richness and depth that brings purpose to every experience and encounter.

> May I draw on the insights that appear to support my evolution.

LOVE YOURSELF THROUGH THE PROCESS

You don't have to wait until you are feeling better, happier, stronger, past the pain or through the change.
You need loving now, so love yourself through the process.

LOVE YOURSELF NOW

So many of us hold the false belief that we have to prove ourselves and our worth before we can receive our own love.

But we need loving now, in the thick of the difficulty, while we are feeling sad, lonely, confused and scared. And the most potent love is the love that comes from our own heart.

We can look to others for love and support, and we should — it's why we're here on this Earth, to connect with and love one another. But we must also develop an unconditional positive regard for our own wellbeing, our own healing and our own journey.

Check in with yourself daily to gauge how you're travelling and then do your best to respond kindly to whatever arises.

Care deeply about what you need and want and then give generously to support your health and happiness.

Value your life and the contribution you make by prioritising the things that bring you meaning and fulfilment.

Appreciate you for you and vow to be loyal to yourself and your unique path.

Now is the time to love you, to nurture you, to care for and support you. Don't wait. You don't have to try, prove, justify, convince or demonstrate your worth. You were born worthy of love and deserve loving now.

> May I find a way to love myself now exactly as I am, where I am.

ALLOW AND ACCEPT

One flaw many of us have is an inability to reach out and accept the help we need.

We can be superstars at giving our time and care to those facing difficulty but often do a rotten job of being on the receiving end.

Somewhere along the way we got the message that asking for help is a sign of weakness, so rather than put our hands up for help, we stoically press on independent of others. By doing so, we block the sustenance we desperately need while denying others the chance to lovingly give.

This fundamental flaw can be corrected at the level of belief.

Noticing what we tell ourselves about our situation and what we make asking for help mean will allow us to accept the support we need.

We all have times we cannot and should not face on our own. And we aren't completely equipped to respond to every challenging situation we come across — that's what friends and family and colleagues and neighbours and sometimes perfectly positioned strangers are for.

Worthiness is the foundation of healthy receiving.

We are all worthy of love and support in whatever form is needed.

Giving does not occur in a vacuum — it is in relationship to and with receiving.

We will all have opportunities to give and we will all have opportunities to receive.

Love yourself enough to allow and accept the help you need.

> May I value myself enough to ask for and receive the help I need.

invest in yourself

Your wellbeing matters. Full stop. Whoever you are, wherever you are, your mental, emotional and spiritual health need to become your priority.

Give yourself what it is you need.

Take a walk, a nap, get a massage, pick up a novel, phone a friend, paint, write, dance, sing — whatever it takes to nurture, nourish, top-up and tend to your own wellbeing. Every day.

BE THE FRIEND YOU NEED

We all know what it's like to feel the discomfort and doubt uncertainty can bring — to have our present disrupted as we face an unknown future and not know where to turn next.

And we've all experienced the healing power of friendship at such times. We've all been that steady shoulder and compassionate ear for another. We've been that loving friend who listens patiently to the crying and the ranting, the one who sits without judgment next to another in their time of suffering.

But too many of us give our friends more love, more care, more help, more respect, than we give ourselves. And that's not okay.

How we treat a dear friend — openly, kindly, with no judgment and no reproach — is how we need to treat ourselves. The affirming words, the warm tone and the interest in their situation — we all deserve that too, from the love within.

We need friendship and connection with others but we must first and foremost belong to ourselves.

We must connect, befriend and love ourselves — our self-esteem depends on it, as does our ability to navigate change with self-compassion. We need to be there for our suffering as it surfaces and hold it gently as we do our best to lessen it, just as we would for a friend.

It's time to be the friend you need.

Whatever it is you require, give it to yourself now. Invest in your health, your wellbeing, your happiness, your present and your future self. You're worth it.

> **May I be a loving and supportive friend to myself.**

DROP THE COMPARISONS

The grass can look so much greener in someone else's paddock. What they've achieved and where they're at can be extremely enviable and seemingly out of our reach.

But we let ourselves down when we judge our journey against others.

We mistakenly think comparing ourselves with another will bring comfort to the discomfort we're feeling about our own perceived lack of progress, when all it does is make us feel worse.

We're not even comparing apples with apples — we're all uniquely designed, complete with our own personal history and circumstances, in different places and stages, with some of us at the beginning of our journey while others are halfway through and going in a totally different direction.

That's why comparing our path to someone else's is futile!

Whether it's another's career, relationship, housing, healing or happiness journey, we undermine our own progress and achievements when we compare our position with someone else's. We rob ourselves of the self-respect we deserve and shatter our self-worth, falling prey to negative self-talk that has us condemning ourselves for all that we are not achieving, doing, feeling or being.

We have our own journey to live — the unique path we are each custom-built for, with its own personalised curriculum designed to support our evolutionary growth.

Comparing yourself to others is detrimental to your wellbeing, and every time you do, you hurt your own heart and risk losing the momentum and commitment you need to continue the next leg of your journey.

> May I respect the path that is my own, and walk it in my own unique way.

press pause

Feelings of overwhelm and fatigue often signal our tolerance has reached its limit.

But we mistakenly think pausing is a sign of weakness. We fear it looks like we don't have what it takes to make it through, or that we've given up, but it's necessary if we are to keep going with our wellbeing intact and our wits about us.

When we pause, we put the issue, the challenge, the situation down, taking our attention off it so we can regain our strength for what is yet to come.

We take a much-needed mental vacation if only for a day, an hour, a breath, to rest and reset so we can regroup and recommit to the next leg of the journey.

PERMISSION TO BE

Where you are right now on the journey, what you're experiencing and what you're feeling is to be acknowledged and accepted. No apologies. There's no need to justify or explain being you, exactly as you are.

Why? Because to validate our experience and our feelings is what initiates the compassion we need during tough times. And because every time you deny your experience and invalidate your true feelings, you abandon yourself.

Whatever we are going through right now —
the upset, the disruption, the difficulty, the pain —
will not disappear just because we've dismissed it
or downplayed its impact.

You matter. Your feelings matter. Your needs matter. Your experience matters. What you want matters. And there's only one person you need permission from to be who you are, where you are. That person is you.

To let yourself be human is the greatest gift you can give yourself, especially during upheaval and uncertainty. The acceptance that comes from the permission you give yourself to be as you are and where you are has the capacity to help and heal.

Seeing and accepting the despair, the pain, the anguish, the struggle — that deep recognition and acceptance of our self, our situation and our suffering — exactly as it is, opens the door to us finding the strength to carry on.

Give yourself the permission you need to be who you are, where you are, with all the fears, tears, hopes and struggles you're feeling right now.

It's the most potent form of self-love you can give and receive.

> **May I give myself permission to be who I am.**

SPEAK WITH CARE

We all speak to ourselves about all sorts of things. There's a commentary running almost non-stop as the mind goes about naming, analysing, reflecting, correcting, judging, preferring, accepting — whenever it wants, about whoever it pleases, ourselves included.

Many comments may go unnoticed, but they do not pass through without harm.

The thoughts you choose and the voice you use have a huge effect, not just on those around you, but on you too!

Your emotional state, your sense of self-esteem and confidence, your belief in yourself and the choices you make, are all affected by the way you speak to yourself about yourself.

When we find ourselves under pressure or struggling with change, our self-talk can go off, criticising, blaming, complaining and shaming us for our feelings and our actions. It'll use anything we have or haven't done against us. And it hurts. We suffer and our ability to cope suffers.

But if we are to make it through this journey consciously, compassionately, connected and empowered, we must become aware of the voice we speak with and listen to.

It matters how you speak to yourself about yourself. And it matters how you speak to yourself about the situation you're in.

It matters because it affects your self-esteem, your wellbeing and whether you can make it through this change in one piece. It matters because you matter, and because this journey is your life. It deserves your wholehearted support, acceptance and love.

It's time to start speaking to yourself like you matter. Because you do.

May I be aware of my voice and use it with care to support me on this journey.

go gently

Force is never a good idea. It just creates tension disrupting any chance we have of being in and connecting with flow and it whittles away our already vulnerable sense of self-esteem.

So whatever you're going through, and growing through, go gently with yourself.

Kindly, softly, lightly. No force —
just a whole lot of gentle love.

USE A TENDER TOUCH

Change can be painful, opening old wounds and creating new ones, but we don't always tend to them tenderly. So often we berate ourselves for having wounds in the first place. We want to ignore them, push past them, pretend they're not even there, telling ourselves to get over it and stop being so sensitive.

But our suffering does not disappear just because we withdraw our attention from it, nor do our wounds heal when they are buried and forgotten.

Our pain, our wounds, our hearts, are crying out for our tender touch — to be patient, kind and gentle, not harsh, critical and dismissive.

Wounds signify our desperate and very human need to be loved and accepted just as we are. When we lack the connection that we crave, are rejected or deemed not good enough, it hurts our hearts deeply and we ache for the healing balm of love.

But we don't like to admit it — we disapprove of and shame ourselves for the wounding we feel.

But that soft spot, that tenderness, that vulnerability needs our tender touch.

With compassionate awareness we can tend to our wounds tenderly.

Honestly and carefully we see what there is to see, holding everything gently with the intention to ease the ache and the pain causing it. We take our time to process what's needed next, choosing thoughtfully who or what will be the most helpful, all the while honouring ourselves and our delicate situation.

Every hurt, every heartache is a call for love and each one needs your tender touch.

> **May I treat my heart tenderly and with compassion.**

HONOUR YOUR JOURNEY

We're all on a journey — but no two are the same. And none are without their heartbreaks and hardships.

In this action-oriented, results-driven world, we often find ourselves focused on the future, eagerly looking to what's next and how far we still have to go, rather than appreciating how far we've already come.

We do ourselves a great disservice when we dismiss all we have lived through and achieved.

To downplay the difficulties, the traumas, the challenges and to discount how much we've grown and how far we've come is to dishonour our struggles and devalue all that we have gained and who we have become as a result.

Honouring our unique path and process helps us to respect our life as well as the personal contribution we have made to it.

Congratulate yourself for all the changes you have successfully navigated and bravely instigated.

Validate the effort you've applied, your commitment to persevering, how you get back up when you've been knocked down, and praise yourself for all that you have faced and healed, forgiven and learnt.

Value the person you have become as a result of life and its many challenges because you are deserving of your own acceptance, approval and appreciation.

This journey is yours.

Respect it and hold it lovingly. Honour all that you have been through to become who you are today.

> **May I honour the journey I am on and value who I have become.**

walk on

Sometimes we don't know how to keep going on the journey of life. But we don't have to know how to do it all now. We just have to take the next step, and then the one after that. One step at a time.

We all know this, but we so easily forget.

Challenging circumstances and the many steps we still have to take can stop us in our tracks. But if we direct our focus on what's right in front of us — the one next step, and only that one — we are on our way to walking.

Walk on, fellow traveller, one conscious and compassionate step at a time.

CONCLUSION

We don't measure how well we've journeyed in terms of speed or distance travelled. It's about what we've learned and unlearned along the way, how well we've managed and who we've become as a result of the changes we have endured and mastered.

Every journey asks something of us. But we can't deliver if we don't show up and face what's being asked with our minds and hearts open.

To find our way successfully, we must move through life consciously and compassionately, meeting and managing each challenge with the intention of coming through it better than we were before — expanded, healed, evolved, strengthened, softened, humbled. To do this, we need to change both our relationship with change and our relationship with ourselves as we go through change.

Remember, there isn't one way — there is only your way. And that will be the way that suits and serves you and your own personal evolutionary journey.

With gratitude...

What a journey this book has been — one that I couldn't have made without the support of so many gifted and loving people.

Sheri McKerrow, you have been on the Seeker & Sage journey with me for several years now, always bringing out the best in me and showing me what was possible. Thank you for helping me to align with my values, my vision and my voice.

Lauren Mitchell, your encouragement to keep going, your writerly wisdom and your editorial eye have helped to not just bring this book to life, but to turn it into a work that enriches the reader experience. I can't thank you enough.

Raelee Tuckerman, your meticulous editing has given this book the professional polish it needed. Thank you for the time and care you have given to me and my words.

Tess McCabe, without you this book wouldn't be the beautiful visual creation that it is. Thank you for your patience, your ideas, and for 'getting me' and what I could see for this book when I couldn't find the words. It has been a joy to collaborate with you.

Amy McKenzie and Danielle Burns, thank you for supporting my work and for so kindly reading those early drafts.

Dearest friends, family, and followers, so many times I doubted myself and my message but there you were with your 'likes' and comments, sharing my words and thanking me for making a positive difference to your day — you have no idea how much your support means to me. Thank you all for encouraging me to stay on the path. And a special shout out to Mum who has never failed to comment on an Instagram post!

Nic, Lauren and Harvey, thank you for loving me just as I am and for helping me to be who I came here to be. My life is all the richer for having you in it.

And then there is Rolly. Your love for me and belief in my mission has never faltered. I am eternally grateful for you and to you and wouldn't want to do life without you. Thank you with all my heart.

And God, who would I be without You. Thank You for EVERYTHING.

ABOUT THE AUTHOR

Gena McLean is a passionate seeker, writer and teacher who supports others to deepen their connection with and experience of the journey of life. Her teachings, workshops and personal growth tool *Note to Self* have already helped thousands to honour their path, trust their innate wisdom and live more authentic and meaningful lives.

Through her dedicated writing practice, she feeds her insatiable appetite for truth and then, with her heartfelt desire to ease the human condition, lovingly shares her discoveries under the name Seeker & Sage — a name which captures who Gena is as well as her orientation to life.

When she's not reading, writing, baking, walking or napping, she's drinking tea and pondering the nature of life and our place in it. She calls the Victorian Goldfields home, where she dwells with her husband, two children and neurotic but adorable Spoodle.

www.seekerandsage.com
Instagram/Facebook @seekerandsage

SEEKER & SAGE—
A PHILOSOPHY,
A VISION

Seeker & Sage is an orientation to life—a way of being that empowers us to live consciously and curiously with the intention to live a deeply meaningful life. It is based on the premise that life is a journey and that along the way we will encounter endless opportunities to awaken, expand, heal and grow.

The Seeker

~ Is the part of us that wants to know—it searches for meaning and truth and understanding in order to live life connected and whole.

~ Is on a journey, navigating the inner terrain in conjunction with and in relation to the outer world.

~ Is curious, inquisitive and reflective toward life and its experiences.

~ Takes a proactive approach to life and is keen to activate and participate in their own healing, expansion, prosperity and fulfilment.

- Is self-aware and conscious of the world around them.
- Practices the qualities of willingness, trust, faithfulness, patience, and openness.
- Believes that life is happening 'for them' not 'to them'.

The Sage

- Is the wisest aspect of us that arises and as a result of the seeking and learning.
- Helps us become more of who we came here to be.
- Strengthens our connection with our intuition, giving us access to guidance and wisdom that is beyond the rational mind — information that can help us live our most potent, authentic and fulfilling life.

Our inner Seeker can lead us to our inner Sage. This is
a continual process of becoming in which we actively
engage with life for this very purpose.

We are each the Seeker and the Sage — the student
and the teacher, the novice and the practised —
simultaneously throughout our life, regardless of the
roles we play and job we do.

It is my heartfelt hope that more and more people
will adopt the approach of a Seeker. That they will
live each day with an orientation of openness and
a curiosity for what's going on within them and
around them; willing to see what there is to see
and know what there is to know; digging deep for
the understanding and meaning within events and
situations; purposefully engaging in their experiences
to live them as fully as they can; learning and growing
as they journey through life; dedicated to becoming
the truest and most authentic them they can be.

ALSO BY THE AUTHOR

Note to Self: Reminders for life's choices
Innovative Resources
ISBN 9 781 920945 407

Note to Self is a set of 24 cards that encourage us to face life's choices honestly and openly. Promoting self-reflection, self-awareness, and self-responsibility, they assist us to think, speak and act in ways that are empowering and supportive, reminding us we have the power to choose and thus, the power to change our experience for the better.

On the front of each card is a statement, prompting and affirming what may have been a long-forgotten truth. On the back are three key questions that invite reflection, contemplation, exploration and possibility.

Choose a card to inspire your day or your week, or turn to the cards for the clarity, direction, or closure you seek, journaling your response and writing your own 'notes to self'.

Published by and available from Innovative Resources: **www.innovativeresources.org**

To read or listen to Gena reflecting on this valuable resource, go to: **seekerandsage.com/note-to-self/**

First published in 2021 by Seeker & Sage, Melbourne, Australia.

© Gena McLean 2021

All rights reserved. No part of this work may be reproduced, stored in a retrieval system, or transmitted in any form or by any means, electronic, electrostatic, magnetic tape, mechanical, photocopying, recording or otherwise without prior permission in writing of the publisher.

A catalogue record for this book is available from the National Library of Australia at catalogue.nla.gov.au

Cover and internal design and layout by Tess McCabe
www.tessmccabe.com.au

Author photo by Morgan McMurtrie.

All web addresses are current at time of writing.

ISBN 978-0-646-83712-3

Printed in Australia.

www.seekerandsage.com
Instagram/Facebook @seekerandsage

DISCLAIMER
The views, opinions and thoughts expressed in this book belong solely to the author and are intended for the purpose of education and entertainment. This book should not be used as a substitute for professional assistance, therapeutic support or medical advice. In the event of physical or mental distress, please consult with appropriate health professionals. The application of ideas and information presented in this book are the choice of the reader, who assumes full responsibility for their understanding, interpretation or results. The author assumes no responsibility for the actions or choices of any reader.

www.ingramcontent.com/pod-product-compliance
Lightning Source LLC
Chambersburg PA
CBHW040741020526
44107CB00084B/2838